What's in this book

This book belongs to

_____

神奇的笔 The magic pen

学习内容 Contents

沟通 Communication

说出文具名称
Say the names of some
stationery items

生词 New words

★ 也	also, as well
★ 纸	paper
★ 笔	pen
★ 铅笔	pencil
★ 橡皮	rubber
★ 尺子	ruler
★ 本子	notebook
★ 文具盒	pencil case
用	to use
恐龙	dinosaur

句式 Sentence patterns

我也有一支神奇的笔。
I also have a magic pen.

浩浩也笑着说。
Hao Hao also says with a smile.

跨学科学习 Project

了解文房四宝，用毛笔写字
Learn the four Chinese treasures of the study and write with a Chinese writing brush

文化 Cultures

中西方绘画风格
Chinese and Western paintings

Get ready

1 Do you think fairy tales can become real?

2 Is there a real magic pen?

3 What would you draw if you had a magic pen?

bǎn zi
本子

qiān bǐ
铅笔

浩浩用铅笔在本子上画恐龙。

晚上，纸上的恐龙变成真的。

wén jù hé

文具盒

xiàng pí

橡皮

恐龙打开文具盒，铅笔
和橡皮掉到地上。

尺子

浩浩用尺子指向它，大叫："回去！"

"是我啊，我是纸恐龙啊！"爸爸笑着说。

"我也有一支神奇的笔！"
浩浩也笑着说。

Let's think

1 Match and retell the story.

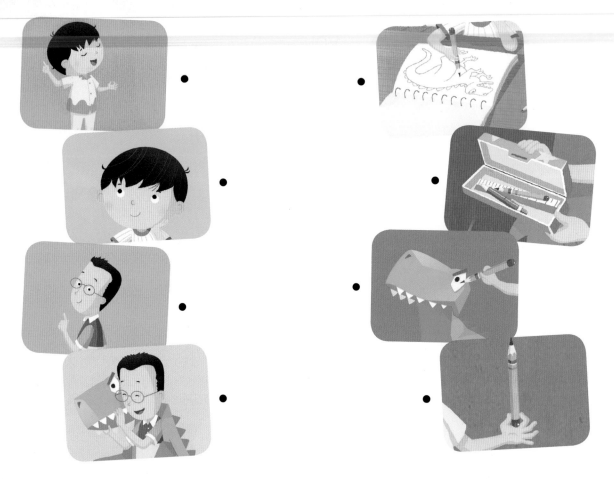

2 Design and draw a magic pen. Talk about it with your friend.

New words

1 Learn the new words.

恐龙　　笔　　铅笔　　尺子　　橡皮

用

本子　　文具盒　　纸

也

2 Look at the picture above and circle the correct answers.

a What stationery items can you see?

铅笔　恐龙　蛋糕　橡皮

b What does Hao Hao want to buy?

本子　纸　文具盒　恐龙

c Ling Ling also wants to buy a dinosaur.
Which character means 'also'?

也　不　是　有

听听说说 Listen and say

🎧 03 **1** Listen and circle the correct answers.

🎧 04 **2** Look at the pictures. Listen to the sto

1 What is Hao Hao doing?

a 看书

b 画画

c 喝果汁

2 What is in the pencil case?

a 尺子

b 本子

c 文具盒

3 What did Hao Hao draw?

a 头

b 鼻子

c 耳朵

4 What did Ling Ling draw?

a 恐龙

b 爸爸

c 妈妈

3 Role-play the dialogue with your friend. Then replace the red words with other words and say.

你好。

你好。

有铅笔吗？

有。你喜欢什么颜色？

我喜欢红色的。

有文具盒吗？在哪里？

也有，在这里。

谢谢。

Task

Check if you have the same stationery as your friend. Complete the table and say.

	尺子	铅笔	文具盒	本子	纸
我也有					
我没有					

Game

Find out what you can put in the pencil case. Say in Chinese.

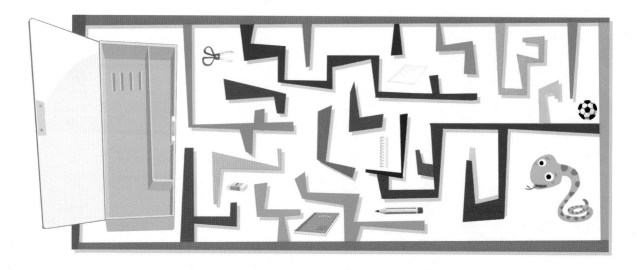

Song

 05 Listen and sing.

我的文具盒，
里面有什么？
铅笔直，尺子长，
用来做什么？
本子上写字，
白纸上画画，
还有橡皮一小块，
天天都用它。

课堂用语 Classroom language

Be quiet.	⚠	(calendar)
安静一点。	请注意。	重要！
Be quiet.	Pay attention.	Important!

写一写 Write

1 Learn and trace the stroke.

斜钩

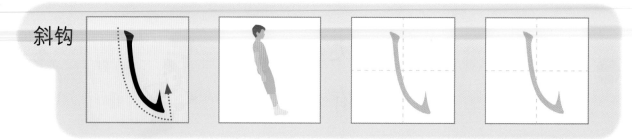

2 Complete ㇄ in the following characters.

我　纸　成　或

3 Find the strokes and trace them with the given colours.

4 Trace and write the character.

纸

纸 纸 纸

5 Write and say.

我们在 □ 上画画。

汉字小常识 **Did you know?**

Many characters are made up of upper, middle and lower components.

Colour the upper component red, the middle component blue and the lower component green.

高 鼻 蕉 茶 黄

1 Chinese and Western paintings have different styles. How do you like them?

Chinese painting is one of the oldest art forms in the world. It is done on rice paper or silk with black ink or coloured pigments.

Oil painting is very popular in Western countries. These paintings are done on canvas with oil paint.

2 Play a bingo game.

Find three animals painted in the same style in one straight line and say their names in Chinese.

1 Do you know the Chinese four treasures of the study? Learn about their functions.

毛笔
Chinese writing brush

墨水
Ink

纸
Paper

砚台
Ink stone

2 Write Chinese calligraphy with the four treasures of the study and say.

我用毛笔在纸上写字。
我也有一支神奇的笔！

1 Throw the dice with your friends and see who can finish the game first.

③ Write 'paper' in Chinese.

④ 你喜欢恐龙吗？

⑤ 尺子

② Miss a turn.

⑥ 你喜欢什么文具？

① 这是什么？

⑦ 这是什么？

⑫ Say 'I draw with a pencil.' in Chinese.

⑪ 你有几支铅笔？

⑧ 你的文具盒里有什么？

⑩ Say 'I also have a magic pen.' in Chinese.

橡皮

⑨

2 Work with your friend. Colour the stars and the chillies.

Words	说	读	写
也	☆	☆	🌶
纸	☆	☆	☆
笔	☆	☆	🌶
铅笔	☆	☆	🌶
橡皮	☆	☆	🌶
尺子	☆	☆	🌶
本子	☆	☆	🌶
文具盒	☆	☆	🌶

Words and sentences	说	读	写
用	☆	🌶	🌶
恐龙	☆	🌶	🌶
我也有一支神奇的笔。	☆	🌶	🌶
浩浩也笑着说。	☆	🌶	🌶
Say the names of some stationery items	☆		

3 What does your teacher say?

My teacher says ...

Words I remember

也	yě	also, as well
纸	zhǐ	paper
笔	bǐ	pen
铅笔	qiān bǐ	pencil
橡皮	xiàng pí	rubber
尺子	chǐ zi	ruler
本子	běn zi	notebook
文具盒	wén jù hé	pencil case
用	yòng	to use
恐龙	kǒng lóng	dinosaur

Other words

神奇	shén qí	magical
变成	biàn chéng	to become
真的	zhēn de	real
打开	dǎ kāi	to open
掉	diào	to drop
地	dì	floor
指向	zhǐ xiàng	to point at
回去	huí qù	to go back
笑	xiào	to smile
说	shuō	to say
支	zhī	(measure word for pens)
啊	a	(a particle used at the end of a sentence to express appreciation or indicate a pause)

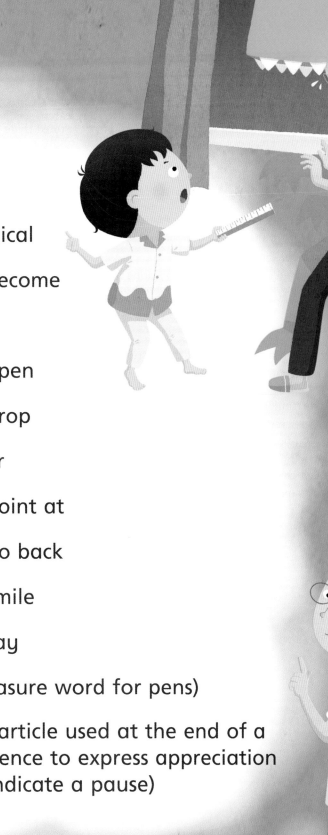

OXFORD
UNIVERSITY PRESS

Oxford University Press is a department of the University of Oxford.
It furthers the University's objective of excellence in research, scholarship,
and education by publishing worldwide. Oxford is a registered trade mark of
Oxford University Press in the UK and in certain other countries

Published in Hong Kong by
Oxford University Press (China) Limited
39th Floor, One Kowloon, 1 Wang Yuen Street, Kowloon Bay,
Hong Kong

© Oxford University Press (China) Limited 2017

The moral rights of the author have been asserted

First Edition published in 2017

Illustrated by Anne Lee, Wildman, KY Chan and KK Ng

Photographs for reproduction permitted by Dreamstime.com

China National Publications Import & Export (Group) Corporation is an authorized distributor of
Oxford Elementary Chinese.

Please contact content@cnpiec.com.cn or 86-10-65856782

ISBN: 978-0-19-082195-1

10 9 8 7 6 5 4 3